Brilliant Skies

Written by P.A. Lin
Illustrated by V.A. Kitsco

Dedicated to John Kitsco

who spent many hours in the sky as an aerial photographer!

Always high above us, the sky is clear and bright.

When day pulls up its blankets, stars fill up the night.

ursa minor
ursa major

Early in the morning, the sunrise lights the sky.

Late into the evening, it sets and says goodbye.

Truth be told, the sun we see never goes away,
But since the Earth is spinning, it just looks that way.
The Earth is spinning towards the east: spinning, spinning, spinning!
So in the east it always seems the day is just beginning.

NORTH
WEST
EAST
south

The peaceful beauty of the morning captivates our eyes.
The colors of the sunrise are always a surprise!

You might see yellow, orange, or pink, maybe even red!
Colors that might remind you of a mighty dragon's head!

Earth's atmosphere is like a prism that bends, refracts the light.
So that we see these colors that bring us great delight.

There are also certain spectacles that take place in the sky.
Great displays of dancing lights frolicking up high!
Close up to the Arctic, these are called the Northern Lights.
Also known as Aurora Borealis, they are truly very nice!

Down by Antarctica, you can see the Southern Lights.
Called Aurora Australis, they are another paradise.

Clouds may look like white marshmallows floating high up in the sky,
But they're actually quite heavy, more like boulders that fly.
When you look upon them, they're never quite the same!
Sometimes heavy and gray, or white, wispy, and tame!

CIRRUS
NIMBUS
CUMULUS
STRATUS

When you see thunderheads, head inside quickly to play.
Whatever you do, get out of lightning's way.
Lightning is dangerous, and it can mean bad luck.
When you hear thunder roar, that means that you could be struck.

The loud roars of thunder might give you a fright,
But viewed from a distance, a storm's a delight.
Streaks of yellow against a backdrop of grey,
It's really spectacular, an electric display!

Brilliant skies of pink, orange, and red.
Look out at the sky before you go to bed.
Maybe you'll see something, something so fine,
Or something quite subtle, a little sublime.

The sky is a mystery of colors and light.

It can look dull and cloudy, or blue and quite bright.

Perhaps full of stars on a clear winter's night.

Even when cloudy, a beautiful sight!

Go outside, or look outside your window. Look up at the sky.
What do you see?
Make a list:

1. ____

2. ____

3. ____

4. ____

5. ____

6. ____

7. ____

8. ____

9. ____

10. ____

Draw a picture of the sky as you look at it:

About the Author:

Patricia A. Lin (B.Sc., B.Ed., M.Ed.) is an educator in Calgary, Alberta, Canada, where she resides with her husband, daughter, and dog. When she is not working or writing, she loves spending time out in nature with her family. She is passionate about topics related to nature and the preservation of the Earth.

About the Illustrator:

Victoria A. Kitsco, a retired teacher with a B.A. and a professional diploma in Education, resides in Edmonton, Alberta, Canada. She has enjoyed art all of her life. She is also an avid gardener and a talented pianist. When she is not gardening or doing art, she loves to spend time with her family, including her granddaughter.

Please note:

All rights reserved, including the right of reproduction in any form, without permission of the author and/or illustrator.

The author can be contacted at plinauthor@gmail.com
The artist can be contacted at VickyArtist70@gmail.com

If you enjoyed this picture book, you may also enjoy these books, written by the same author, and illustrated by the same artist:

Incredible Trees

A Mother's Love

Amazing Oceans

Also be sure to check out P.A. Lin's
Awesome A-Z Nature Word Searches

Remember to consider posting a review on Amazon if you enjoyed the book!

Namaste ☺